# EXTREME!

# Fingerprint Wizards

## The Secrets of Forensic Science

## Ross Piper

*press*

Mankato, Minnesota

Fact Finders is published by Capstone Press,
a Capstone Publishers company.
151 Good Counsel Drive, P.O. Box 669,
Mankato, Minnesota 56002.
www.capstonepress.com

First published 2008

Produced for A & C Black by

Monkey Puzzle Media Ltd
The Rectory, Eyke, Woodbridge
Suffolk IP12 2QW, UK

Library of Congress Cataloging-in-Publication Data

Piper, Ross.
    Fingerprint wizards : the secrets of forensic science / by
Ross Piper.
        p. cm. -- (Extreme!)
    Includes bibliographical references and index.
    Summary: "An introduction to forensic science
procedures including the examination of fingerprints,
DNA, gunpowder, fibers, and handwriting found at a
crime scene"--Provided by publisher.
    ISBN-13: 978-1-4296-3117-4 (hardcover)
    ISBN-10: 1-4296-3117-1 (hardcover)
    ISBN-13: 978-1-4296-3137-2 (softcover)
    ISBN-10: 1-4296-3137-6 (softcover)
1. Fingerprints--Identification--Juvenile literature.
2. Forensic sciences--Juvenile literature 3. Criminal
investigation--Juvenile literature. I. Title.

HV6074.P57 2009
363.25--dc22

2008029215

Editor: Cath Senker
Design: Mayer Media Ltd
Picture research: Shelley Noronha and Lynda Lines
Series consultant: Jane Turner

This book is produced using paper that is made from
wood grown in managed, sustainable forests. It is natural,
renewable, and recyclable. The logging and manufacturing
processes conform to the environmental regulations of
the country of origin.

Printed in the United States of America

Picture acknowledgements
Alamy p. 18 right (Louise Murray); Corbis pp. 6 (Bill
Fritsch/Brand X), 19 (Jeremy Horner), 26 (Steve Klaver);
Georgia Bureau of Investigation p. 24; Getty Images pp. 5
(Patti McConville), 7, 9 (AFP), 15 (AFP), 28 bottom (AFP),
29; iforensic.com p. 28 top; Rex Features p. 17 (Denis
Closen); Science Photo Library pp. 1 (Paul Rapson), 4 (Paul
Rapson), 8 (Tek Image), 10 (Paul Rapson), 11 (Alfred
Pasieka), 12 right (Gustoimages), 13 (Alfred Pasieka), 14
(Volker Steger/Peter Arnold Inc), 16 (Mauro Fermariello), 18
left (Jim Varney), 21 (Philippe Psaila), 22 (Andrew Lambert),
23 (Geoff Tompkinson), 25 (Mauro Fermariello); Topfoto pp.
20 (Photonews), 27 (Photonews). Artwork on p. 12 left by
Tim Mayer.

The front cover shows computer artwork of a glowing
human handprint (Science Photo Library/ Alfred Pasieka).

Every effort has been made to contact copyright holders
of material reproduced in this book. Any omissions will be
rectified in subsequent printings if notice is given to the
publishers.

# CONTENTS

**Abbreviations** **m** stands for meters · **ft** stands for feet · **cm** stands for centimeters
**in** stands for inches

# Fantastic forensics

At first, some crimes look impossible to solve. Fortunately, there is a special kind of investigator who helps the police find clues that ordinary people would never see. This investigator is called a forensic expert.

Forensics is the use of science to help solve crimes. Forensic experts are among the first people at a crime scene. They hunt for evidence and carefully take it back to the forensic science laboratory. They try to work out what happened and help to trace the criminals.

## Evidence everywhere

Evidence can be a tiny fiber of clothing, a piece of paper left at the crime scene, or even a single strand of hair.

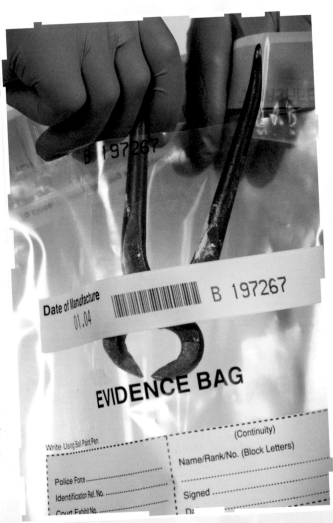

*Every piece of evidence is placed in a separate plastic evidence bag.*

EVIDENCE BAG

Date of Manufacture
01.04

B 197267

Write Using Ball Point Pen

(Continuity)

Name/Rank/No. (Block Letters)

Police Force

Identification Ref. No.

Signed

Court Exhibit No.

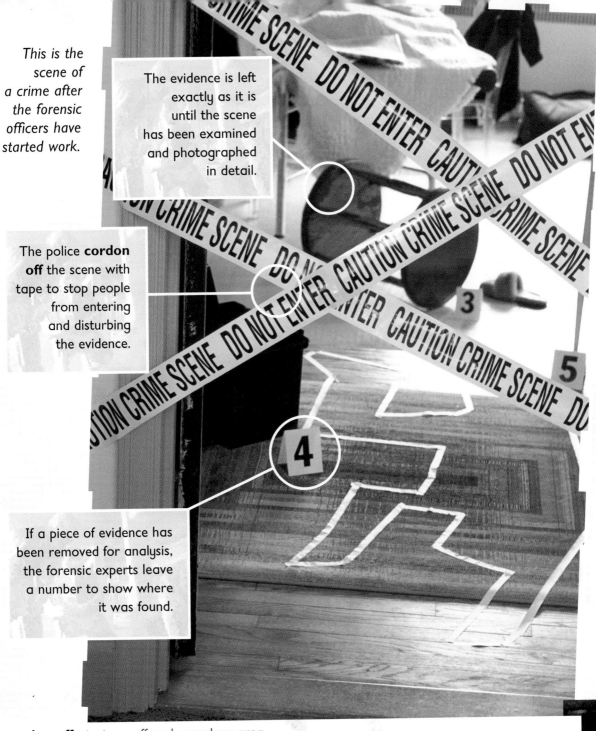

*This is the scene of a crime after the forensic officers have started work.*

The evidence is left exactly as it is until the scene has been examined and photographed in detail.

The police **cordon off** the scene with tape to stop people from entering and disturbing the evidence.

If a piece of evidence has been removed for analysis, the forensic experts leave a number to show where it was found.

**cordon off**   to tape off and guard an area

# The forensics team

Once a major crime has been discovered, the scene is soon filled with people dressed in white suits and masks. Each of these forensics experts has a special job to do.

Some of the experts take photos or videos to record the crime scene exactly as they found it. Others collect evidence. This could range from clothing to fingerprints, blood, scraps of paper and fabric, and even tiny fibers on the floor or walls.

*The forensic photographer takes many photos from different angles at the crime scene.*

**contaminating**   making something impure by adding a polluting substance

# Patient and sharp eyed

The most important skills for the forensic experts are patience and careful observation. It can take hours, days, or even weeks to collect all of the evidence at a crime scene.

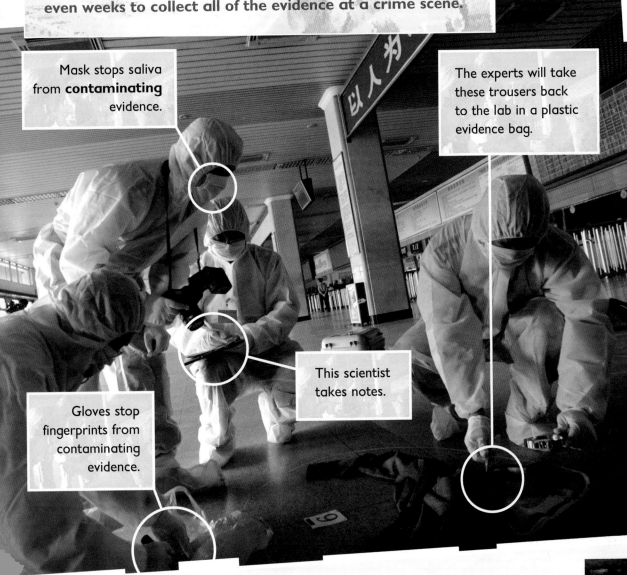

Mask stops saliva from **contaminating** evidence.

The experts will take these trousers back to the lab in a plastic evidence bag.

This scientist takes notes.

Gloves stop fingerprints from contaminating evidence.

*These forensic experts in China are training to deal with bombings. They search for chemical evidence after an explosion.*

# Breaking and entering

This robber smashed the glass door of a house using a hammer and reached in to unlock the door from the inside.

Imagine being a forensics expert who has been called to the scene of a big robbery. One of the first things the police will want to know is how the robbers got in. The thieves may have broken in or had help from people inside.

Investigators look for a variety of clues. Some are simple. If there is glass under a broken window inside the building, the window must have been broken from the outside. The experts also examine locks and alarms to see if they have been damaged.

## Quick getaway

Banks are protected by alarms and cameras. Once inside a bank, the robbers have only a few minutes to grab the money before the police arrive.

Photographers taking pictures of a tunnel after a bank robbery in Brazil. Thieves dug the 260-ft (80-m) tunnel under the neighboring houses.

The tunnel was roughly 2.3 ft (70 cm) square and had its own lighting system.

The tunnel was 13 ft (4 m) deep and came up under the bank.

The thieves had to break through steel-reinforced concrete to break into the bank.

# Sticky fingers

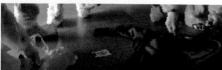

A forensics expert's main job is to find information that can help the police to identify the criminals. One of the best ways to do this is to find fingerprints.

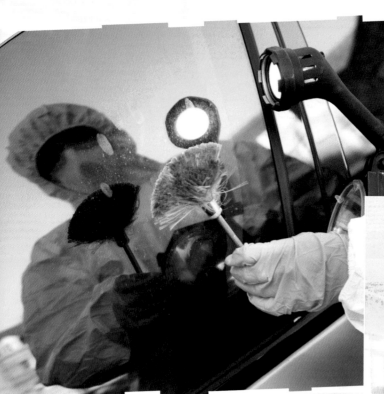

Everyone's fingerprints are unique—unlike anybody else's. If criminals have touched objects at the crime scene, the police can use the fingerprints to prove the **culprits** were there.

*This forensics officer wipes dust over the car window so the fingerprints show up.*

## Fingerprint fraudsters

Some criminals went to great lengths to cover up their fingerprints. A few even had skin **grafted** on to their fingertips from elsewhere on their body.

**culprits** people who have done something wrong

10

Of course, fingerprints can come from innocent people as well as criminals. The forensic experts take fingerprints from everyone who might have left some at the crime scene: the people who work there, regular visitors, the cleaners, and so on. Any fingerprints that don't belong to these people might have come from the criminals.

This is a tented arch.

These are whorl patterns.

This is an arch with a loop above it.

Loops are the most common pattern.

*Fingerprints are made up of different patterns. This computer illustration shows colored fingerprints.*

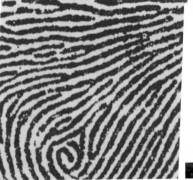

**grafted**   moved from one part of the body to another using surgery

# DNA fingerprints

**Fingerprints are not the only way to identify criminals. DNA can also be used. Almost everyone has unique DNA.**

*When DNA is analyzed, it forms patterns. Can you see which suspect's DNA matches the DNA at the crime scene in this simplified diagram?*

Our bodies are made up of around 10 trillion cells. Nearly every one of these cells contains tightly coiled DNA in the center.

A criminal may leave hairs, skin cells, or tiny drops of blood at the crime scene. Each of these contains DNA. Forensic experts can analyze them to find the criminal's **DNA fingerprint**. The DNA fingerprint can be compared to DNA samples from suspects.

| DNA at crime scene | Jeff | Tom | Anna | Kim |
|---|---|---|---|---|

*A forensic scientist takes a sample from a suspect's mouth to collect cells for DNA fingerprinting.*

**DNA fingerprint**   the unique pattern formed from pieces of DNA

This computer illustration shows a **molecule** of DNA, some DNA sequences, and DNA fingerprints.

# Code for life

DNA is the instruction book for all living things. It contains the codes that determine how you grow, how you look, and many other things, too. Apart from identical twins, no two people have the same DNA.

DNA is made up of two spirals.

Linking these two spirals are four chemicals (shown colored blue, yellow, red and green) that form pairs.

The sequence of these chemicals is the genetic code.

**molecule** a microscopic string or group of linked atoms

# Explosive evidence

## Having a blast

Make your own mini-explosion. Drop a chewy mint candy into a glass of cola. Lots of gas is produced very quickly, and the cola quickly bubbles out of control like a little volcano. **A real explosion is the same—but much, much bigger and faster!**

Some of the clues a forensic expert gathers might not lead straight to the criminal. Yet they can still help the police track down their target.

After an explosion, for example, forensic experts may find traces of the **detonator**. They may be able to tell the police what kind of detonator set off the explosion. The police compare it to the types of detonator used by different criminal groups. This will help them work out which group carried out the crime, and may lead them to the criminals.

*These are different kinds of explosives, including semtex (green) and TNT (brown).*

**detonator**  device used to set off an explosion

14

A forensic expert collects evidence at the scene of a bomb explosion.

Explosives release huge amounts of gas very quickly. They cause an intense jolt, lots of noise, and extreme heat.

A piece of the detonator has survived the blast.

Tiny traces of the explosive are left on the ground.

# Strands of evidence

Even the tiniest piece of evidence can help the police identify a criminal. A single hair, for example, will contain a robber's DNA. Strands of fiber can also provide clues.

At every crime scene there are tiny strands of fiber from clothes and other fabrics. Most of these are useless to the police, but one or two may have been left behind by a criminal. Forensic experts can often work out what the culprit was wearing. Later, the fibers can be matched to the person's clothes to show that he or she was at the crime scene.

*These microscope images show close-ups of strands of fiber. They were found in a bathroom where a crime took place.*

## Finding fabrics

**Forensic experts find tiny strands of fabric using ultraviolet (UV) and infrared lights and even vacuum cleaners!**

**infrared light** light at the red end of the spectrum (the colors that make up light)

To understand how forensic experts work, try collecting strands of fiber from clothes and furniture in your home.

Using tweezers, place each strand in a separate evidence bag. Look at the fibers with a magnifying glass or microscope. Compare them to fibers from your family's clothes. Who has been in your room? Forensic experts work in this way to try to find evidence linked to a suspect.

*These forensic scientists use UV light to find strands of fiber on these trousers.*

The spray reflects UV light, showing where the fibers are.

Orange glasses make it even easier to see the reflected UV light.

This man uses a spray that sticks to single fibers.

**ultraviolet (UV) light** light at the blue end of the spectrum

# Trails and tracks

Near many crime scenes, tire tracks and footprints are left in soft soil or mud. These can provide valuable clues for a forensic investigator.

*A forensics officer holds the plaster cast of a footprint found at the scene of a crime.*

*A forensic expert collects evidence from a car tire.*

## Make a footprint mold

Make a running and walking footprint in soft soil. Pour liquid **plaster of Paris** into both types of footprint and let the liquid set. Carefully remove the molds. Do they look different?

**WARNING!**
You MUST ask an adult to help you with this activity.

**plaster of Paris**   a white powder that is mixed with water to make a paste that sets hard

Forensic experts take lots of photographs and make molds from the footprints and tire tracks. From footprints, they can work out the likely height and weight of the person. Soil from the crime scene will be in the tread of the criminal's car tires and shoes. Experts examine the car and shoes of the suspects to look for a match.

The tracks show the direction in which the car was moving.

The tire tracks show the type of car and the tires it has.

The footprints show the size of the owner's feet and the type of shoes he or she was wearing.

# Written evidence

Most people's handwriting is unique. Expert investigators looking at several different examples of handwriting can usually say whether they were all written by the same person or not.

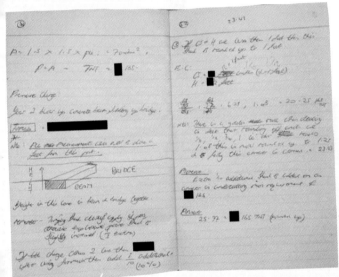

This means handwriting samples can often be used as evidence. Forensic handwriting experts can show that a ransom demand, or a note on how to disable an alarm system, was written by a particular person—even if he or she denies it.

*These notes are about preparing and placing explosives. Experts analyzed them and proved they had been written by Dhiren Barot. He was sent to prison for terrorism.*

# Invisible writing

If the suspect writes on a notepad, the writing will leave an imprint on the sheet underneath the note. Forensic experts can see these imprints using a special machine. It charges the paper with **static electricity** and makes black powder stick to the imprint.

**static electricity**   the electrical charge produced by friction

Forensic experts also search for invisible evidence on written notes. They may find the criminal's fingerprints, DNA from skin cells, or DNA from saliva if the person licked an envelope to send a letter.

*This forensic scientist looks for fingerprints to find out who touched the letter.*

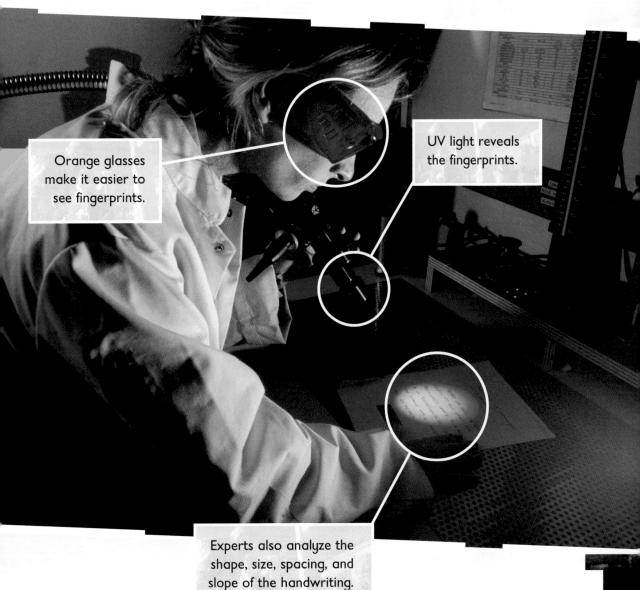

Orange glasses make it easier to see fingerprints.

UV light reveals the fingerprints.

Experts also analyze the shape, size, spacing, and slope of the handwriting.

**Even if it cannot be read, a tiny scrap of paper from a crime scene might provide investigators with an important clue.**

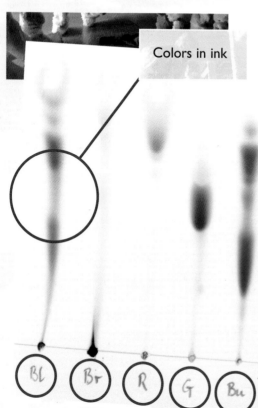

Colors in ink

BL    Br    R    G    Bu    O

Pens have different inks that give them their color. Using **chromatography**, forensic experts can separate these inks to make an individual pattern. Then they can compare the ink in a handwritten note with ink from pens in the suspect's home.

*With paper chromatography, you can see how different inks separate into the pigments (substances used as coloring) that make them up.*

From left to right: black, brown, red, green, blue, orange.

# Try out chromatography

Cut out five strips of paper towel. Using different markers, make a spot ½ inch (1 cm) from the bottom of each strip. Stick each strip to a piece of straight wire. Dip the end of each strip in water. The water rises up the strip and separates the pigments.

**chromatography**   separation of a substance into separate parts

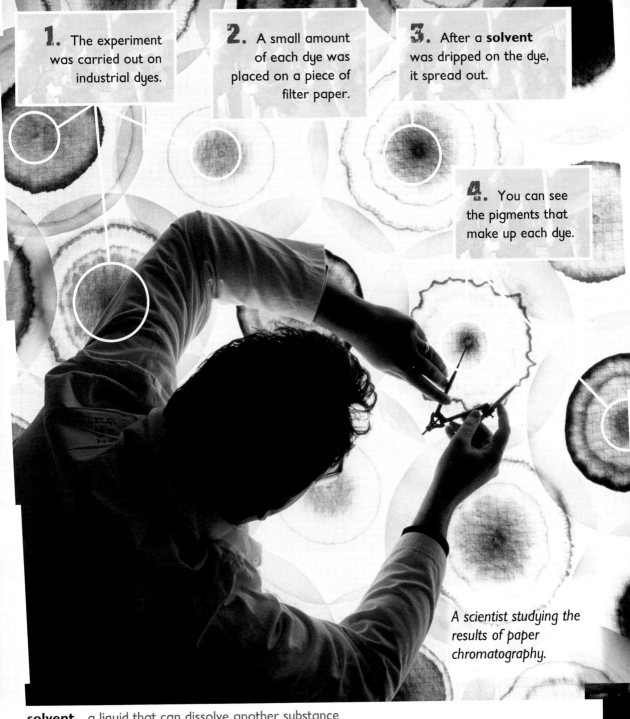

1. The experiment was carried out on industrial dyes.

2. A small amount of each dye was placed on a piece of filter paper.

3. After a **solvent** was dripped on the dye, it spread out.

4. You can see the pigments that make up each dye.

*A scientist studying the results of paper chromatography.*

**solvent** a liquid that can dissolve another substance

# Magnificent microscopes

Microscopes are one of a forensic investigator's main tools. Almost everything that is brought back to a forensic lab is examined, a tiny piece at a time, using a microscope.

The **lenses** in a microscope allow forensic experts to find tiny pieces of evidence that are invisible to the naked eye. They might see minute strands of fabric from the culprit's clothes. If the suspect has carried explosives, tiny particles may have become caught in the fabric. Forensic scientists can see them with a microscope.

*When a weapon is fired, smoke from the burning gunpowder surrounds the hand of the shooter. Tiny amounts of powder are left on the hand. This means that a forensic expert can figure out if a person has fired a gun.*

## Microscopic

An electron microscope can magnify tiny things 2 million times and can even show the surface of individual bacteria cells. These are so small that 1,000 of them could fit end-to-end on a pinhead!

**lenses**   specially shaped pieces of glass or plastic that can bend and focus light to magnify objects

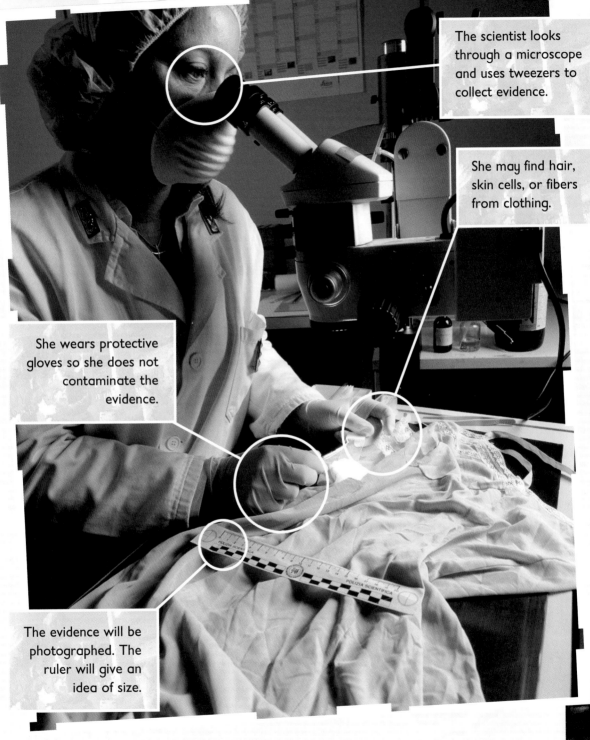

The scientist looks through a microscope and uses tweezers to collect evidence.

She may find hair, skin cells, or fibers from clothing.

She wears protective gloves so she does not contaminate the evidence.

The evidence will be photographed. The ruler will give an idea of size.

*This forensic scientist examines a dress from a crime scene.*

# Caught on camera

Crime scene investigators sometimes get help from **CCTV** cameras. If they're lucky, the cameras might even have filmed the criminal's face.

CCTV cameras work 24 hours a day, filming important places and areas where crime is likely to occur. Modern cameras can record what happens in great detail. Some can film in complete darkness using infrared light.

*This CCTV camera scans the cafeteria at a high school in New Jersey.*

## The streets have eyes

In these countries, people are most watched by CCTV and other **surveillance** forms: the United Kingdom, Singapore, Malaysia, Russia, and China.

**CCTV** closed circuit television, which continually videos an area to protect it from crime

After a crime, the police and forensic experts examine the CCTV recordings to look for evidence.

This is CCTV footage of an armed robbery in southern England in 2006. The robbers stole more than $105 million (£53 million) from a Securitas depot.

Although the robbers wear balaclavas, the images help police to identify them.

One of the robbers left a mask with his DNA in a van containing stolen money.

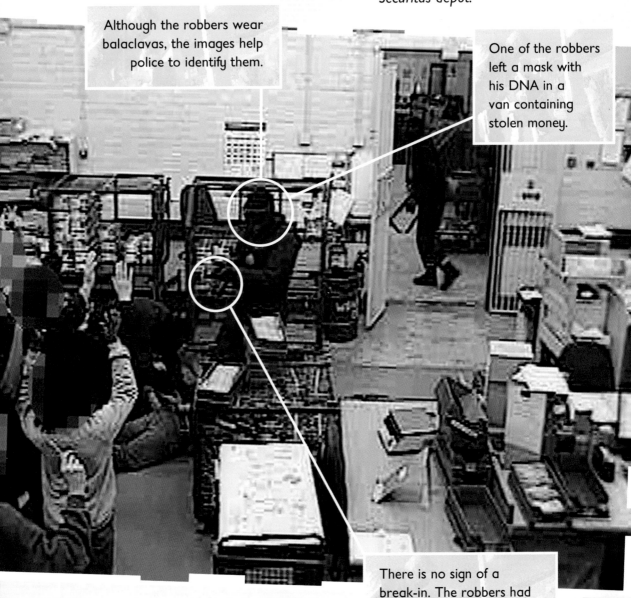

There is no sign of a break-in. The robbers had forced the staff at gunpoint to open the depot.

**surveillance** watching a place where crime may occur

# The evidence puzzle

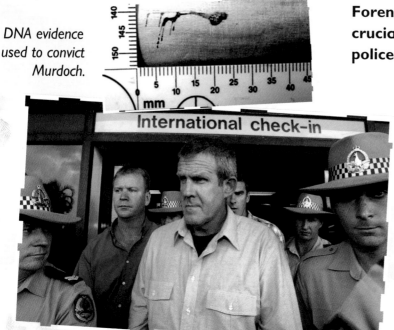

*DNA evidence used to convict Murdoch.*

**Forensic science can provide crucial evidence to help the police to capture criminals.**

By using DNA fingerprinting and analyzing substances found at the crime scene, the police can be nearly certain they have caught the right person. Yet they do not rely on science alone. They also use other information, such as **eyewitness** statements and databases with details of known criminals.

*Australian Bradley John Murdoch (center) was found guilty of murdering British tourist Peter Falconio in 2001. Forensic scientists had found his DNA fingerprint at the crime scene.*

## DNA tricks

**Some criminals have tried to beat the DNA experts. In 1992 Dr. John Schneeberger committed a crime, but police could not match his DNA to the DNA found at the crime scene. To fool the testers, he had surgically inserted a pipe filled with another man's blood into his arm.**

**eyewitness** person who sees something happen

Sometimes criminals even provide evidence against themselves. Hidden in the memories of their computers are emails and other information proving they took part in a crime. Police often take the computers of suspects away to analyze this stored information.

*A police officer removes a computer from the home of a murder suspect.*

The police will examine the files on this computer's hard drive for clues that might help them find the killer.

29

# Glossary

**CCTV** closed circuit television, which continually videos an area to protect it from crime

**chromatography** separation of a substance into separate parts

**contaminating** making something impure by adding a polluting substance

**cordon off** to tape off and guard an area

**culprits** people who have done something wrong

**detonator** device used to set off an explosion

**DNA fingerprint** the unique pattern formed from pieces of DNA

**eyewitness** person who sees something happen

**grafted** moved from one part of the body to another using surgery

**infrared light** light at the red end of the spectrum (the colors that make up light)

**lenses** specially shaped pieces of glass or plastic that can bend and focus light to magnify objects

**molecule** a microscopic string or group of linked atoms

**plaster of Paris** a white powder that is mixed with water to make a paste that sets hard

**solvent** a liquid that can dissolve another substance

**static electricity** the electrical charge produced by friction

**surveillance** watching a place where crime may occur

**ultraviolet (UV) light** light at the blue end of the spectrum

# Further information

## Books

**Crime Scene Detective: Using Science and Critical Thinking to Solve Crimes** by Karen Schulz (Dorling Kindersley, 2007)
This book challenges you to observe carefully, organize and record data, think critically, and conduct simple tests to solve crimes.

**Crime Scene Detective: Become a Forensics Super Sleuth, with Do-It-Yourself Activities** by Carey Scott (Dorling Kindersley, 2007)
Activities to help you to become a super-sleuth.

**Crime Scene Investigations: Real-Life Science Activities for the Elementary Grades** by Pam Walker and Elaine Wood (Jossey Bass, 2007)
Neat tricks and simple techniques for careful observation and the collection of evidence.

**Eyewitness: Forensic Science** by Chris Cooper (Dorling Kindersley, 2008)
Discover the ground-breaking methods scientists use to solve crimes. Includes CD-ROM and charts.

**Forensic Science** by Alex Frith (Usborne Publishing Ltd, 2007)
Information about the science and methods that forensic experts use to collect evidence.

**Forensics** (Kingfisher Knowledge) by Richard Platt (Kingfisher, 2008)
Discover how to read the signs left by a criminal, find the evidence, and learn what goes on in the crime laboratory.

**Investigating Murder Mysteries** by Paul Dowswell (Heinemann, 2004)
About the forensic techniques used in murder investigations—includes case studies.

**Investigating Thefts and Heists** by Alex Woolf (Heinemann, 2004)
Discusses how some famous robbery cases were solved using forensic science.

## web sites

FactHound offers a safe, fun way to find Internet sites related to this book. All of the sites on FactHound have been researched by our staff. Visit *www.facthound.com* for age-appropriate sites. You may browse subjects by clicking on letters, or by clicking on pictures and words.
**FactHound will fetch the best sites for you!**

# Index

# GRANDES PERSONAJES EN LA HISTORIA DE LOS ESTADOS UNIDOS™

# ABIGAIL ADAMS

## DESTACADA PRIMERA DAMA

**MAYA GLASS**

TRADUCCIÓN AL ESPAÑOL:
TOMÁS GONZÁLEZ

The Rosen Publishing Group, Inc.
**Editorial Buenas Letras**™
New York

Published in 2004 by The Rosen Publishing Group, Inc.
29 East 21st Street, New York, NY 10010

Copyright © 2004 by The Rosen Publishing Group, Inc.

**First Spanish Edition 2004**
First English Edition 2004

**Cataloging Data**

Glass, Maya
[Abigail Adams: Destacada Primera dama.]
Abigail Adams : Destacada Primera dama / Maya Glass.— 1st ed.
    p. cm. — (Grandes personajes en la historia de los Estados Unidos)
Summary: Introduces the life of Abigail Adams, the wife of President John Adams, who was much more independent than many women of her time, running a farm in her husband's absence and speaking and writing about women's rights.
Includes bibliographical references and index.
ISBN 0-8239-4124-8 (lib. bdg.)
ISBN 0-8239-4218-X (pbk.)
6-pack ISBN 0-8239-7558-4
1. Adams, Abigail, 1744–1818—Juvenile literature. 2. Presidents' spouses—United States—Biography—Juvenile literature. 3. Adams, John, 1735–1826—Juvenile literature.
[1. Adams, Abigail, 1744–1818. 2. First ladies. 3. Women—Biography .5. Spanish language materials.]
I. Title. II. Series: Primary sources of famous people in American history. Spanish.
E322.1.A38 G55 2004
973.4'4'092—dc21

*Manufactured in the United States of America*

**Photo credits:** cover, pp. 4, 5, 9, 10, 13 courtesy of the Massachusetts Historical Society; p. 7 courtesy of Map Division, The New York Public Library, Astor, Lenox, and Tilden Foundations; p. 8 courtesy of the Rhode Island Historical Society; p. 11 © A.G.K., Berlin/SuperStock Inc.; pp. 12, 21 (top) National Portrait Gallery, Smithsonian Institution/Art Resource, NY; pp. 15, 21 (bottom) Library of Congress Geography and Map Division; p. 17 © Burstein Collection/Corbis; pp. 18, 22 National Archives and Records Administration; p. 19 Pennsylvania Academy of the Fine Arts, Philadelphia/The Bridgeman Art Library; pp. 23, 26 © Hulton/ Archive/Getty Images; p. 25 Independence National Historical Park; p. 27 (top) Picture Collection, The Branch Libraries, The New York Public Library, Astor, Lenox, and Tilden Foundations; p. 27 (bottom) © Bettmann/Corbis ; p. 29 U.S. Department of the Interior, National Parks Service, Adams National Historic Park.

Designer: Thomas Forget; Editor: Mark Beyer; Photo Researcher: Peter Tomlinson

# CONTENIDO

# 1  UNA MUJER EXCEPCIONAL

Abigail Adams fue la esposa de John Adams, el segundo presidente de Estados Unidos. A la mujer del presidente se le llama "primera dama". Abigail Adams vivió durante un período muy interesante de la historia. Además fue la madre de John Quincy Adams, quien en 1825 se convirtió en el sexto presidente del país.

Retrato al óleo de John Adams. John conoció a Abigail Smith en 1759. Se escribieron muchas cartas antes de casarse en 1764.

Retrato de Abigail Adams en 1766. Ya entonces era una mujer resuelta. Su marido tomaba muy en serio sus opiniones.

Cuando Abigail era joven, Estados Unidos aún no era un país. Durante su vida se libró la Guerra de Independencia. En ella, un grupo de colonias se liberaron de Gran Bretaña y crearon los Estados Unidos de América. John Adams viajaba con frecuencia para ayudar a construir el país. Abigail le escribió muchas cartas cuando él estaba lejos de casa.

## ¿SABÍAS QUE...?

A John y a Abigail Adams les gustaba escribirse cartas. En las cartas él a veces la llamaba "Señorita Adorable".

En este mapa de 1783 aparecen los primeros trece estados.
Abigail y John Adams fueron patriotas norteamericanos. Ambos
querían que las colonias se independizaran del gobierno británico.

En sus cartas, Abigail expuso sus ideas sobre la esclavitud y los derechos de las mujeres. Estas cartas son importantes documentos históricos de Estados Unidos. Abigail Adams habló contra lo que creía equivocado. No muchas mujeres hacían eso en aquella época. En aquel entonces se consideraba que las ideas de las mujeres no eran iguales a las de los hombres. John Adams hablaba con Abigail de todos los temas.

Retrato de Deborah Sampson de la época de la Guerra de Independencia. Deborah Sampson también fue una mujer resuelta. Era tan patriota que se vistió de hombre para luchar en la guerra.

the House and Furniture of the Solisiter General have fallen
a prey to their own merciless party — Surely the very fiends
feel a reverential awe for virtue & patriotism, whilst they
Detest the parracide & traitor —

I feel very differently at the ap
proach of Spring to what I did a month ago. We knew not
then whether we could plant or sow with Safety, whether when
we had toild we could reap the fruits of our own industry, whether
we could rest in our own Cottages, or whether we should not
be driven from the sea coasts to seek shelter in the wilderness,
but now we feel as if we might sit under our own vine
and eat the good of the land — I feel a gaieti de Coar
to which before I was a Stranger, I think the Sun looks
brighter, the Birds sing more melodiously, & nature puts on
a more chearfull countanance. We feel a temporary
peace, & the fugitives are returning to their deserted habitations

tho we felicitate ourselves, we sympa
thize with those who are trembling least the Lot of Boston
Should be theirs — They cannot be in Similar circumstances
unless pusillanimity & cowardise Should take possession of
them — They have time & warning given them to see
the Evil & shun it — I long to hear that you have de
clared an independancy — and by the way in the new
Code of Laws which I suppose it will be necessary for you
to make I desire you would Remember the Ladies, &
be more generous & favourable to them than your ancestors
do not put such unlimited power into the hands of the
Husbands. Remember all Men would be tyrants if they
could. if perticuliar care & attention is not paid to the
Ladies we are determined to foment a Rebellion, and will
not hold ourselves bound by any Laws in which we have
no voice, or Representation — That your Sex are Naturally
tyrannical is a Truth so throughly established as to admit of no
dispute, but such of you as wish to be happy willingly give up the
harsh title of Master for the more tender & endearing one of Friend

Carta de Abigail a John Adams. En ella le pide que tenga en cuenta los derechos de las mujeres. John se disponía a participar en la preparación de la primera Constitución.

# 2 PRIMEROS AÑOS

Abigail Smith nació el 11 de noviembre de 1744. Abigail quería ir a la escuela pero nunca pudo hacerlo. Leía libros y revistas y escribía un diario. Después conoció a John Adams, con quien compartía el amor por el conocimiento. John y Abigail se conocieron en 1759. Empezaron a escribirse, compartieron sus ideas en las cartas y se enamoraron.

Ésta es una de las primeras cartas de John Adams a Abigail Smith. En ella puede verse lo alegres que se mostraban cuando se escribían. Como John a menudo estaba lejos de casa, se comunicaban por carta.

Cuando era niña, Abigail no recibió una educación formal. De las niñas se esperaba que aprendieran a cocinar, coser, criar niños y atender a las visitas. Pero Abigail leyó numerosos libros y encontró muchas maneras de educarse.

John y Abigail se casaron en 1764. John Adams era abogado y además tenía una granja en Massachusetts. Le gustaba estar con Abigail y trabajar en la granja. En 1765 tuvieron una niña a la que llamaron Nabby. En 1772 Abigail tenía ya cuatro hijos más. Abigail disfrutaba criando y educando a sus hijos.

John Quincy fue uno de los hijos de la familia Adams. John se educó en la escuela y también en el hogar. De su madre aprendió la importancia de los derechos de las mujeres.

Dibujo de la granja de la familia Adams en Braintree, Massachusetts. Abigail se encargó de la granja durante los años en que John estuvo trabajando en Europa.

Muy pronto la familia se mudó a Boston. John quería dedicarle más tiempo a la política. Gran Bretaña estaba imponiéndoles fuertes impuestos a las colonias. Uno de los productos gravados con impuestos era el té. Abigail pensaba que este impuesto era injusto y en su casa decidió servir café, en lugar de té.

---

## LA LUCHA CONTRA EL IMPUESTO AL TÉ

Catorce hombres lucharon contra el impuesto al té. Vestidos como indios norteamericanos, lanzaron cajas de té británico a la bahía de Boston. A este hecho se le conoce como la Fiesta del Té de Boston *(Boston Tea Party)*.

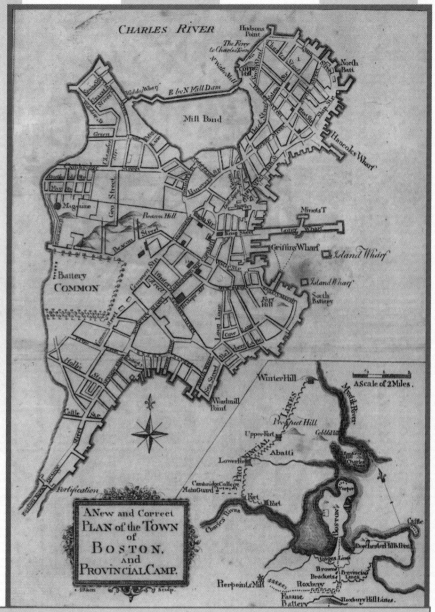

Mapa de Boston, Massachusetts, la ciudad más grande de Nueva Inglaterra. Gran parte del trabajo preparatorio de la Guerra de Independencia se hizo en Boston.

# **3** VIDA POLÍTICA

Muchos norteamericanos pensaban que las colonias debían gobernarse a sí mismas. A estas personas las llamaban "patriotas". A las personas que querían seguir siendo parte de Gran Bretaña las llamaban "realistas". Abigail y John Adams eran patriotas. Abigail recibió a muchos patriotas importantes en su casa y se hizo amiga de Thomas Jefferson y Benjamin Franklin.

## ¿SABÍAS QUE...?

Benjamin Franklin era muy amigo de Abigail Adams. Sin embargo, Ben Franklin y John Adams no simpatizaban.

Thomas Jefferson escribió la Declaración de Independencia. Conocía a John y a Abigail Adams. Abigail recibía en su casa a Jefferson y a otros Padres de la Patria.

John Adams dejó la carrera de abogado para dedicarse a la política. Se hizo miembro del Congreso Continental. Este grupo ayudó a escribir la Declaración de Independencia y la Constitución. La Guerra de Independencia comenzó en 1775. John Adams viajó durante gran parte de aquel año.

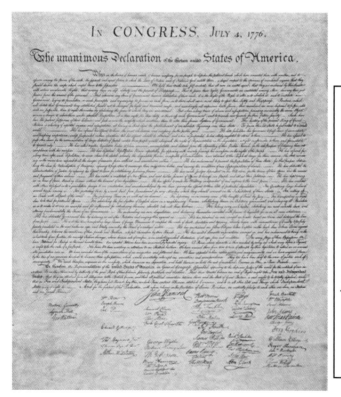

En la Declaración de Independencia se hacía la lista de las razones por las cuales las colonias querían independizarse de Gran Bretaña. John Adams firmó el documento en 1776.

Retrato de Benjamin Franklin, 1782. Franklin ayudó a escribir la Declaración de Independencia y la Constitución. Era escritor e inventor.

En 1778, John Adams trabajó en Francia. Luego de una breve visita a su hogar, regresó a Francia donde permaneció por cinco años. Abigail Adams se hizo cargo del hogar mientras su esposo estuvo fuera. Se encargaba de muchas tareas que las mujeres de la época por lo general no hacían. Estaba a cargo de la granja y del dinero del hogar. Abigail convirtió también su casa en hospital para los soldados heridos en las batallas.

## AHORRANDO DINERO DURANTE LA GUERRA

Para ahorrar dinero, Abigail Adams tenía que fabricar a mano muchos de los artículos que su familia necesitaba. Entre ellos estaban los vestidos y el jabón.

A John Adams *(derecha)* no le gustaba separarse de Abigail. Sin embargo, tenía que hacerlo, cuando viajaba, pues había dedicado la vida a su país. Abigail le escribió muchas cartas mientras él estuvo en Francia *(mapa)*.

# 4 PRIMERA DAMA

En 1783 terminó la Guerra de Independencia. Abigail Adams se unió a su esposo en Francia. En esos días viajar era difícil. ¡El viaje de Boston a Inglaterra duraba cuatro semanas en barco! La hija de Abigail, Nabby, viajó con ella. La familia Adams permaneció en Europa hasta 1788. Durante su estancia, trataron de mejorar las relaciones entre Gran Bretaña y Estados Unidos.

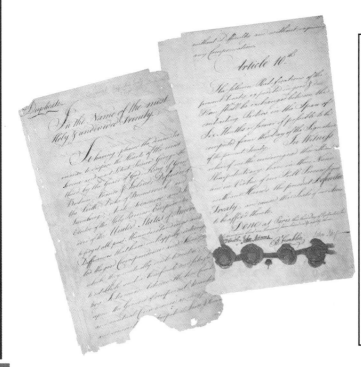

En 1783 se firmó el Tratado de París entre Gran Bretaña y Estados Unidos. Este tratado ponía fin a la Guerra de Independencia y Abigail pudo reunirse con su marido en Francia.

Abigail Amelia Adams Smith (1765–1813) era hija de Abigail y John Adams. La llamaban "Nabby". Nabby se casó con William Stephens Smith en 1786.

En 1789, la familia Adams viajó a Nueva York. George Washington había elegido a John Adams para el cargo de vicepresidente de Estados Unidos. Abigail Adams se hizo buena amiga de Martha Washington. Martha era la primera dama en esa época.

## ¿SABÍAS QUE...?

Abigail compró una casa sin decírselo a John Adams. En esa época las mujeres no podían comprar propiedades. Abigail tuvo que usar el nombre de John para comprar la casa.

En esta pintura de 1795 aparece la primera dama, Martha Washington. Fue la esposa del primer presidente de Estados Unidos, George Washington.

# 5 UNA VOZ A FAVOR DEL CAMBIO

Abigail Adams fue una mujer independiente. Era madre y además trabajaba, en una época en que esto era poco común. Criaba a sus hijos y también manejaba la granja de la familia. Cuando se maneja una granja hay que tomar muchas decisiones. Abigail contrataba a los trabajadores y se ocupaba de la venta de las cosechas.

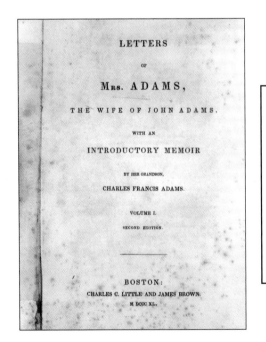

En 1840, después de su muerte, se publicaron algunas de las cartas de Abigail. Ellas muestran lo mucho que trabajó en favor de la educación, de los derechos de las mujeres y en contra de la esclavitud.

LISPENARD'S MEADOWS.
Taken from the N.E. cor of the present Broadway & Spring St.
Drawn by A. Anderson, 1785.

Bocetos que muestran la vida en las granjas en el siglo XVIII. Manejar una granja exigía mucho trabajo. Abigail crió a sus hijos y manejó con éxito la granja de la familia Adams.

Durante su vida, Abigail Adams no vio un gran cambio en lo que se refiere a los derechos de las mujeres. Sin embargo, fue una voz a favor del cambio. Habló y escribió sin descanso a favor de los derechos de las mujeres.

Abigail murió de una enfermedad pulmonar el 28 de octubre de 1818. Tenía casi setenta y cuatro años de edad. Años más tarde, muchas de sus ideas se hicieron realidad.

## LA CONTINUACIÓN DE LA OBRA

El hijo de Abigail, John Quincy Adams, habló siempre en contra de la esclavitud. De su madre aprendió a tratar a todas las personas con respeto.

Abigail Adams murió en su cama en 1818, rodeada por su familia. Había sido esposa de un presidente y madre de otro. Abigail fue una verdadera revolucionaria.

# CRONOLOGÍA

1744—Nace Abigail Smith.

1764—Abigail se casa con John Adams.

1765—John y Abigail tienen una niña, Nabby.

1767—Nace John Quincy Adams.

1768—Nace Susanna Adams.

1770—Nace Charles Adams. Susanna Adams muere en febrero.

1772—Nace Thomas Boylston Adams.

1785—La familia Adams vive en Francia. John Quincy regresa a Estados Unidos. John, Abigail y Nabby se mudan a Inglaterra cuando John es nombrado enviado de Estados Unidos ante Gran Bretaña.

1784—Abigail y Nabby viajan a Inglaterra.

1789—John y Abigail viajan a Nueva York.

1790—John y Abigail se mudan a Filadelfia.

1797—John Adams se convierte en el segundo presidente de Estados Unidos.

1818—Muere Abigail Adams.

# GLOSARIO

**abogado(-a)** Persona que da consejos relacionados con la Ley y habla en representación de otros en los tribunales.

**Congreso Continental (el)** Grupo formado por unos cuantos hombres de cada colonia y que tomaba decisiones en representación de ellas.

**Constitución (la)** Las reglas básicas con las que se gobierna Estados Unidos.

**esclavitud (la)** Sistema en el cual unas personas son "dueñas" de otras.

**Guerra de Independencia (la)** La que libraron por la independencia los soldados de las colonias contra Gran Bretaña entre 1775 y 1783.

**independiente** Libre del control de otros.

**literatura (la)** Escritos de un período determinado.

**política (la)** Forma como trabaja el gobierno.

## SITIOS WEB

Debido a las constantes modificaciones en los sitios de Internet, Rosen Publishing Group, Inc. ha desarrollado un listado de sitios Web relacionados con el tema de este libro. Este sitio se actualiza con regularidad. Por favor, usa este enlace para acceder a la lista:

http://www.rosenlinks.com/fpah/aada

## LISTA DE FUENTES PRIMARIAS DE IMÁGENES

**Página 4:** Retrato de John Adams, de Benjamín Blyth, 1766. Actualmente se encuentra en la Sociedad Histórica de Boston, Massachusetts.

**Página 5:** Retrato de Abigail Adams, de Benjamín Blyth, 1766. Actualmente se encuentra en la Sociedad Histórica de Boston, Massachusetts.

**Página 7:** Mapa de Estados Unidos, 1783. Actualmente se encuentra en la Biblioteca Pública de la Ciudad de Nueva York.

**Página 8:** Retrato de Deborah Sampson, 1797, aproximadamente. Actualmente se encuentra en la Sociedad Histórica de Rhode Island.

**Página 9:** Carta de Abigail a John Adams, escrita el 31 de marzo de 1776. Actualmente se encuentra en la Biblioteca del Congreso, Washington, D.C.

**Página 10:** Carta de John a Abigail Adams, 1762 aproximadamente. Actualmente se encuentra en la Biblioteca del Congreso, Washington, D.C.

**Página 11:** Retrato sin fecha de Abigail Adams.

**Página 12:** Retrato de John Quincy Adams, de Izaak Schmidt, 1783. Actualmente se encuentra en la Institución Smithsonian, Washington, D.C.

**Página 13:** Dibujo titulado *Lugares de nacimiento de John Adams y John Quincy Adams, Braintree, Mass.*, de Elizabeth Susan Quincy, 1822. Actualmente se encuentra en la Sociedad Histórica de Boston, Massachusetts.

**Página 15:** Mapa de Boston de Robert Aitken, grabado, 1775. Actualmente se encuentra en la Biblioteca del Congreso, Washington, D.C.

**Página 18:** La Declaración de Independencia, 1776. Actualmente se encuentra en los Archivos Nacionales, Washington, D.C.

**Página 19:** Retrato de Benjamín Franklin por Joseph Wright, 1798. Actualmente se encuentra en la Academia de Bellas Artes de Pensilvania, Filadelfia, Pensilvania.

**Página 21:** *(arriba)* Retrato de John Adams por Gilbert Stuart, 1798 (finalizado en 1828 por Jane Stuart). Actualmente se encuentra en la Institución Smithsonian, Washington, D.C.

**Página 21:** *(abajo)* Mapa de Francia coloreado a mano por Alexis Jaillot, 1724 aproximadamente. Actualmente se encuentra en la Biblioteca del Congreso, Washington, D.C.

**Página 25:** Retrato al óleo de Martha Washington de Charles Willson Peale, 1795. Actualmente se encuentra en el *Independence National Historic Park*, de Filadelfia, Pensilvania.

**Página 26:** Portada de las *Cartas de la Sra. Adams*, esposa de John Adams, publicadas en 1840 por *Little and Brown*, Boston, Massachusetts.

**Página 27:** *(arriba)* Dibujo de A. Anderson titulado *Lispenard's Meadows*, 1785. Actualmente se encuentra en la Biblioteca Pública de la Ciudad de Nueva York.

# ÍNDICE

# ACERCA DEL AUTOR

Maya Glass es escritora y editora. Vive en la ciudad de Nueva York.